MW00932628

DON'T BE PENNY WISE & DOLLAR FOOLISH

By Andrew McNair

DON'T BE PENNY WISE AND DOLLAR FOOLISH

TABLE OF CONTENTS

Myth #1
"In retirement I won't need as much money"

7

Myth #2
"I am going to pay fewer taxes in the future"

11

Myth #3
"I am not going to live that long"

17

Myth #4
"I am healthy now and my family will take care of me in the future"

23

Myth #5
"I don't need insurance anymore... I am self-insured"

27

Myth #6
"I have to have everything paid off before retirement"

31

Myth #7
"I have to maximize my contributions to my 401 (K)"

35

The title of this book, "Don't Be Penny Wise and Dollar Foolish," originates from an old English citation: "Penny wise is often pound foolish." This proverb is a great basis for the book because, as humans, upon embracing an idea or an institution, we tend to perceive it as fact or as indisputable. As you already know, this can create a dilemma. It's like being caught clinging to an imaginary stronghold while at the top of a ladder and the ground beneath you begins to move. There in lies the problem many Americans are facing today. The sad reality is change will occur over time. Institutions or philosophies, which we adhere to with all our strength, are not doctrines. Therefore, they may have an expiration date stamped on them because they're time sensitive. What works today will most likely not work for long in the future. Unfortunately, this turns my stomach as I write this. Why? Because I know all the variables (such as taxes, inflation, etc.) that I consider while planning someone's financial future are going to be wrong. So what should we do? Quit planning and do nothing? Of course not. The key is planning with relentless accountability. The best way to comprehend great financial planning is to visualize being the captain of a ship. If you're the captain of the ship and you steer your ship to go North and then forget about it, don't expect your ship to keep going in a Northerly direction for long or it may hit some unexpected rocks. If your crew finds out that's how you captain the vessel, you might find yourself walking the plank. Yet that's exactly what millions of Americans do. They get their jobs right out of college and then read a few money magazines advising them to save 10-15% of their income. The only dilemma is in the years to come, while they continue to save, they are actually only saving the same amount as when they started right out of college without accurate adjustments. See, just like navigating the ship, you must continually stay proactive in maintaining, guiding, and planning your financial plan all the way to your goal. If you do that, your ship will find itself arriving at the destination you planned and on time. I hope you enjoy reading this book and uncovering "seven major myths of retirement debunked."

Frank & Ernest: © Thaves / Dist. by United Feature Syndicate, Inc.

"Don't simply retire from something;
have something to retire to."

- Harry Emerson Fosdick

DON'T BE PENNY WISE AND DOLLAR FOOLISH

Myth #1

"In retirement I won't need as much money" } 1

What the World Says:

"You may need between 60% and 80% of your final working years' salary."

-Yahoo Money

Who honestly wants less money? Ideally no one! I understand that it may be necessary for you to have to cut back, but why plan to do this if we don't have to. I often read the same magazines and listen to the same experts, and I hear them advise that you only will need 65% of your income when you retire. Why do we believe this rhetoric? I want at least 100% of my income, and preferably, I would even like a pay raise! I think we deserve to receive what we worked 30 years for and now have a seven-day weekend to enjoy. This is a great example of our culture's mind set regarding the scarcity of wealth. We plan on having a more abundant retirement and, if we intentionally plan on it, then it is statistically proven that you will have a better chance of materially realizing it.

The Reality:

You will most likely need more money in retirement! Many people's houses are not paid off like they originally planned. In fact, most people have refinanced their home over three times before paying it off! Their kids did finally move out, but now they have another whole litter called grandkids to take care of. The expenses never seem to go away, and maybe they shouldn't. In retirement, shouldn't you expect to get a pay raise because now you're free to finally do what you wanted to do all the time? Retirement should be a seven-day week not a two-day weekend. In retirement, many would like to travel, and that costs money.

The Bottom Line:

1

Don't plan for failure; plan for success. Ralph Waldo Emerson once said: "Shoot for the moon. Even if you miss it you will land among the stars." That's my philosophy, too. It's better to have more money than you expected than work your whole life and then be disappointed that your finances are limiting the enjoyment of your much-deserved retirement.

Frank & Ernest: © Thaves / Dist. by United Feature Syndicate, Inc.

"In this world nothing can be said to be certain, except death and taxes."

- Benjamin Franklin

DON'T BE PENNY WISE AND DOLLAR FOOLISH

Myth #2

"I am going to pay fewer taxes in the future" and they're too high right now!

}

2

What the World Says

"After you retire, you'll likely be in a lower tax bracket and be able to keep more of what you've accumulated."

- info.firstinvestors.com

The Reality:

Have you ever heard your CPA, the buddy at the water cooler or any other financial source say, "Tax defer your money because you'll have less income and, therefore, be in a lower tax bracket when you retire." This is hogwash!

Concerning this topic, I like to ask people one question: "Do you feel tax rates are going to be higher or lower in the future?" On either political side of the proverbial fence 99% of the time people say taxes will, more than likely, be higher in the future, and they're probably right. Today, we're at historical lows. Looking at the graph on the next page you will notice the average top marginal bracket from 1913 to 2010 is 59.49%. As I am writing this book, the top marginal tax rates are 35% and will be increasing to 39.6% in 2011. Unfortunately, I expect tax rates to go even higher because, at our current pace, there is no way a government can continue to offer the support it has historically provided without raising taxes or redistributing revenue. Before we get into a tangent on politics, let's go back to our original myth.

Oh, how people quickly forget! The income tax was created as a "temporary" tax to pay for the Spanish American War. So, 98 years later, this temporary tax, or whatever that means, must not be so temporary! It was added to the Constitution as the 16th amendment and enacted on February 3, 1913.

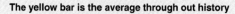

The yellow bar is the average through out history

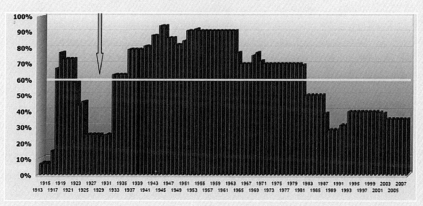

Let's look at the top marginal tax bracket. It has been over 90% fourteen times in its history! The government was also swift to add and implement the withholding tax at the end of WWII in 1945. This act turned out to be a sadly forgotten trick the government played on those poor souls having to also endure a global economic depression and is now passed down to us today. This act enabled the government to begin a mandatory deduction of your paycheck to ensure the government receives its share. It was a great "fast one" they pulled on us because it allowed them to siphon even more money without us becoming suspicious. Before this, people would write large checks at the end of the year to the IRS. It is a lot harder writing a large check to the government versus just letting a small percentage of your paycheck be deducted each month. Isn't it interesting that when Ronald Reagan received his first million dollar movie deal for "Bedtime for Bonzo," in the early '50s, his top marginal tax bracket was 90%. Now, looking at the early '80s, when he was in office, you see what the new tax bracket was ... I guess he remembered!

The Bottom Line:

Unfortunately, because America's average savings for the first time in history was negative in 2006, and even though we're hoarding money (not saving it) from 2009 to 2011, right now we can't even get our saving percentage into double digits. This means less independence, which equates to government assistance. Any form of government funded assistance will cost money and most likely will come directly out of our pockets. This is why there's a great chance you're not going to be paying fewer taxes when you retire, but more!

Frank & Ernest: © Thaves / Dist. by United Feature Syndicate, Inc.

"Let us endeavor so to live that when we come to die even the undertaker will be sorry."

- Mark Twain

Myth
#3

"I am not going to live that long" } 3

What the World Says

"People tend to underestimate how long they are likely to live by more than five years."

- Nottingham University

The Reality:

We are all living a long time. At the turn of the 20th century the average life span was only 47 years! Today, if you're less than 65 years old, there is a greater than 50% chance you or your spouse will reach the age of 92. Furthermore, a baby girl's life span born today is almost 120. This is a great thing because we're blessed with advancing medical technology. The problem lies with how our financial system was engineered. As we have seen in the last couple decades, pensions have become a thing of the past and Social Security will not continue to stand without the government being forced to increase taxes or lower benefits.

3

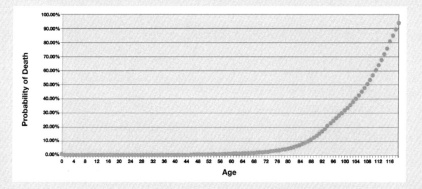

Sadly, there are many people out there who are trying to get the information out that while people are living longer, they are doing it the wrong way. The graph above is a popular graph of probability of death by age. I think we should look at the graph in a more positive manner. Let's look at these same figures but in a more optimistic way. The graph below is your life probability, which is the probability you're going to be around longer than your parents or grandparents were. We believe this is a better and less morbid way of looking at this subject. Look at the figures; there is almost an 80% chance (if you're a female) that you will reach the age of 94. On the other hand, I hate it for us guys because there is only 74% who will reach 94!

3

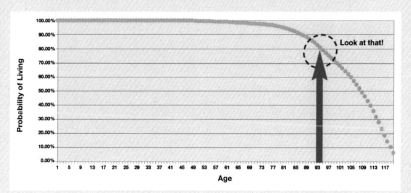

The Bottom Line:

Face the facts. Be glad you are going to see your grandchildren grow up, and maybe you'll even see the day you become a great grandfather or great grandmother. With that in mind, don't overlook your finances and make a note in your plan that there is great chance you will continue to be around longer than your parents were; make sure you're financed to handle it.

3

Arlo & Janis: © United Feature Syndicate, Inc.

"The soul is born old but grows young. That is the comedy of life. And the body is born young and grows old. That is life's tragedy."

- Oscar Wilde

DON'T BE PENNY WISE AND DOLLAR FOOLISH

Myth
#4

"I am healthy
now and my
family will take
care of me in
the future"

}

4

What the World Says

"Acknowledge you'll most likely take on caregiving responsibilities someday."

- health.usnews.com

4

Do you honestly want to become a burden on your family? Obviously the answer is no. However, many people come to this crossroad and convince themselves and/or are convinced by their family that they will not become a burden. Unfortunately, many times this is not the case. As our final days draw near, our needs can grow exponentially. Thankfully, there are options available to us today that will take care of tomorrow. You can make these arrangements for yourself well in advance and more economically than in the future. Don't just "hope" that you and/or your family will have the time or resources to do this for you. Also, how do you know or have the faith that your family will have the resources needed in the future to take care of these unforeseen needs? Have you ever considered long-term care insurance? Too many people view these products as a waste of money, but like any other product it's just a tool that has its place under certain circumstances. A pawn is not a bad piece on a chess board, but if you're looking to jump over other pieces, it is the wrong choice to make. I personally feel that certain products are only needed on very specific cases. Let's look at an ideal case. Take a 60 year old with $300K in assets. To date, the average stay in a nursing home is from two-and-one-half years to three years. The average costs may vary anywhere from $30,000-$75,000 per year. If a 60 year old happens to spend three to four years, spending $65,000 per year, what happens to his plans?

Now he's down to only $105,000, and that's supposed to help him make it to the end? Instead of worrying if you can afford to live much longer, you should be enjoying your final years with those you love most, never becoming a burden to anyone.

The 5 LTC Stress Test

1. Where do you want to live and how much will that cost?
2. Who do you really want to take care of you?
3. How would you like to be cared for should you became terminally ill or incapacitated?
4. If you have a spouse and a child, what level of care would you like provided to them?
5. It's your money, so do you want it depleated or left to future generations?

4

The Bottom Line:

Make sure you are confident about your answers to the 5 LTC Stress test. Also, be sure to take advantage of all the resources and information out there and challenge them all. Find an elder law attorney or estate attorney and make sure they are proponents of coordinating your plan with your financial adviser. These are issues that cannot be handled single handedly by any one professional.

"*I detest life-insurance agents; they always argue that I shall some day die, which is not so.*"

- Stephen Leacock

Myth #5

"I don't need insurance anymore... I am self-insured" }

5

What the World Says
"Better Plan...become self insured."
-Dave Ramsey

I have no idea where this concept came from, but it has been popularized lately by all the "financial gurus." I have yet to see a truly "self-insured" individual. How can you be certain you have enough assets available, liquid enough, to take care of your family in the orderly fashion you would like to, because, in the U.S. today, only around 82% of people have life insurance coverage and many do not even have close to the right amount of coverage their family really needs. This is supported by the fact that only 38% of Americans feel they have enough coverage. Many people have been sold a life insurance policy. The problem lies in that no one has ever asked them what is their life insurance plan? The point is, we can all buy the same products, but if we don't have a strategy surrounding them, they're useless. Take for instance a 50- year-old man living on $75,000 a year income who only has $750,000 of life insurance and no savings or survivor benefit on his pension. If he dies tomorrow, what happens?

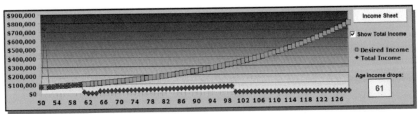

If his wife continues to live her life and sustain their current standard of living, she would run out of money in less than 11 years. Perhaps you are thinking to yourself right now that your spouse only needs 65% of your previous income to live comfortably. Okay, your husband, wife and/or dependents would still run out of money in 17 years, and your assumptions about their standards of living may be incorrect. Maybe they can leave it up to chance and play the lottery.

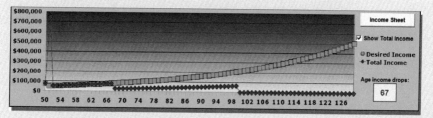

The Bottom Line:

5

There are very few individuals out there who are technically "self insured." Today's typical retiree still has consumer debt, a mortgage, is still helping out their children and maybe the grandkids, too. Sadly, they only ended up with a half-decent pension or 401 (k) with a few hundred thousand in it. Then, when they receive the bill in the mail for their life insurance, they view it as an expense and try justifying eliminating it. The truth is don't be so quick to stop paying for your life insurance in retirement because there are very few systems out there that can accurately validate if you are "self-insured" or not.

That is the reality of the situation. Let's forget this for a second though and move on to the next myth.

The Born Loser: © United Feature Syndicate, Inc.

"*Sign on bank: We can loan you enough money to get you completely out of debt.*"

- *Anonymous*

Myth #6

"I have to have everything paid off before retirement"

6

What The World Says:

"Retire Without a Mortgage...
Paying off your home loan sooner
frees up a lot of cash later."

- AARP

The Reality:

That's what you think! There is a major difference between being in debt and having debt. I have seen too many people struggle to pay off all their debt just for peace of mind. But is this peace of mind worth thousands of dollars of wealth? That's up to you! Ideally, wouldn't you like to be as efficient as possible with your money, and then determine how much peace of mind you can afford? Unfortunately, there is another agenda being pushed on us by the financial gurus of our time. Actually, these "gurus" are right; too many families are enslaved to consumer debts. But, there is a definite difference between consumer debt and having a mortgage. A mortgage is tied to an asset compared to a credit card or any other consumer debt. Also, mortgages and other liabilities tied to assets are offset by the fact that assets such as real estate tend to appreciate. On the other hand, consumer debt, like that couch you bought on your credit card, tends to depreciate. See, freedom doesn't come from everything being paid off but in simply having enough liquid cash on hand to take

6

care of any unexpected emergency. This is where true peace lies. There will always be bills with or without debts.

The Bottom Line:

Try to pay off your debts in a timely order. Don't be enslaved by your debts, but don't let the shackles of trying to pay them off steal your joy. There has to be balance. The secret of the rich is the ideal way of paying off debt is creating real wealth faster.

6

RETIREMENT PLANNING

FORGET A 401K PLAN. WHAT YOUR ACCOUNT NEEDS IS A NINE-ONE-ONE PLAN.

THAVES

Frank & Ernest: © Thaves / Dist. by United Feature Syndicate, Inc.

"I'm not sure I want popular opinion on my side -- I've noticed those with the most opinions often have the fewest facts."

- Bethania McKenstry

Myth #7

7

"I have to maximize my contributions to my 401 (K)" }

What The World Says

"And if you took advantage of catch-up contribution limits ..."

- Kiplinger

No you don't! The sad reality for many people is they finally realize they have not been saving nearly enough for retirement and hit 50 wondering what to do. The truth is not much! The problem lies in the tax law of compound interest. It is old money, not new money, that is essential to compound interest. Under current tax law as of 2010, the law allows for an additional $5,500 catch-up provision after you reach 50 or older. This can be on top of your total yearly contribution of $16,5000. Let's investigate this together and eliminate the opinions. Look at the numbers! Instead of adding another $5,500 to your contributions how about for the last five years before retirement, you stop all together. Am I nuts? Your retirement might suffer horrifically? No, look at what happens!

Years	Deposits	Compound 1	No Deposits for last 5 Years
1	$105,000	$112,000	$112,000
2	$110,000	$124,840	$124,840
3	$115,000	$138,579	$138,579
4	$120,000	$153,279	$153,279
5	$125,000	$169,009	$169,009
6	$130,000	$185,839	$185,839
7	$135,000	$203,848	$203,848
8	$140,000	$223,118	$223,118
9	$145,000	$243,736	$243,736
10	$150,000	$265,797	$265,797
11	$155,000	$289,403	$289,403
12	$160,000	$314,661	$314,661
13	$165,000	$341,688	$341,688
14	$170,000	$370,606	$370,606
15	$175,000	$401,548	$401,548
16	$180,000	$434,657	$434,657
17	$185,000	$470,083	$470,083
18	$190,000	$507,988	$507,988
19	$195,000	$548,548	$548,548
20	$200,000	$591,946	$591,946
21	$205,000	$638,382	$638,382
22	$210,000	$688,069	$688,069
23	$215,000	$741,234	$741,234
24	$220,000	$798,120	$798,120
25	$225,000	$858,988	$858,988
26	$230,000	$924,118	$919,118
27	$235,000	$993,806	$983,456
28	$240,000	$1,068,372	$1,052,298
29	$245,000	$1,148,158	$1,125,959
30	$250,000	$1,233,529	$1,204,776

Where the contributions stop!

7

Look at the difference
$1,233,529 - $1,204,776 = $28,753

Let's investigate the numbers to better understand them. The green column titled "Compound 1" is an individual that for 30 years contributed $5,000 at 7%. On the other hand, the yellow column labeled, you guessed it, "No deposits for last 5 years," is an individual that for only 25 years contributed $5,000. The difference between the two though is only $28,753. So why waste your time and money? Do something more valuable than looking at your IRA balance for the last five years and start spending more money on your family. With the resulting savings, you could take the $5,000 every year for the last five years and go on a cruise or spend a few weeks in Europe with your wife (and even bring the kids too, if you want).

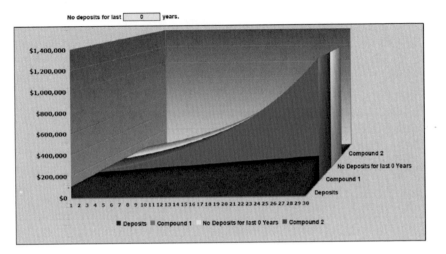

The Bottom Line:

7

Don't pull out your hair! There is no easy 1 -5 year fix that can improve what you have done for the last 30 years financially. The only thing you can do now is enjoy what you have accumulated and meet with a financial professional that can find the inefficiencies in your model and adjust it to give you a better standard of living for the future.

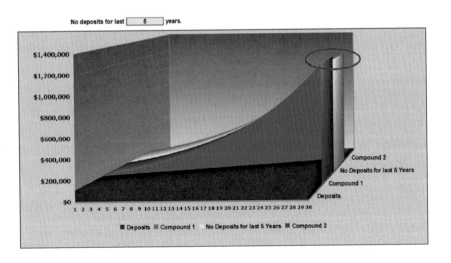

Life Insurance Stats:
http://www.lifeinsurance-selling.com/Exclusives/2010/9/Pages/LIAM-More-stats-resources-and-a-free-realLIFEstories-Web-cast.aspx

Comics:
Comics.com

Quotes:
Thinkexist.com

Graphs:
David L. Anderson

Mortality Table:
Social Security

What the World Says
1. http://finance.yahoo.com/how-to-guide/retirement/18303

2. http://info.firstinvestors.com/docs/pdf/think1st-0899.pdf

3. http://health.usnews.com/health-news/articles/2007/11/02/15-things-you-can-do-to-keep-mom-and-dad-at-home.html

4. http://www.daveramsey.com/article/the-truth-about-life-insurance/lifeandmoney_insurance/

5. AARP, http://www.aarp.org/work/retirement-planning/info-07-2010/retire_without_mortgage.html

6. The Catch Up Guide To Retirement By Kiplinger, http://www.kiplinger.com/features/archives/a-catchup-guide-to-retirement.html

Epilogue

After reading this book, I hope that you are inspired to use more skepticism and to challenge all new ideas. Don't take the "fevers of the week" for face value. Of course, professionals need to disclose everything and be as enthusiastic about the cons as they are about the pros. But it's your responsibility to ask the questions and voice your concerns. The true source to the misconceptions and myths that remain out there is simply laziness. Instead of assuming your financial adviser or best friend knows what they're talking about, be more proactive. Proactive? That's right! Do your due diligence and research these strategies, theories and products before ever signing any check.

"Sacred cows make the best hamburger."

- Mark Twain

Made in the USA
Lexington, KY
01 September 2018